Autism Spectrum Disorders

WELLS EMERY

Copyright © 2014 by Wells Emery

All rights reserved. This book or any portion thereof may not be reproduced or used in any manner whatsoever without the express written permission of the publisher except for the use of brief quotations in a book review

CONTENTS

1 Introduction 1

2 Autism at a Glance 3

3 Going In-Depth 21

4 Living with Autism 41

5 Being Proactive 65

6 Famous People with Autism 69

7 A Few Words in Closing 73

INTRODUCTION

In their eyes are sharp contrasts of colors, in their ears is a confusing cacophony of deafening sounds much like the continuous rustle of leaves, and in their skin is the maddening feel of coarse cotton fabric. For some of them, the world is seen as if through a filter: blurring the details, the social chitchat falling against the dead walls of a soundproof room, or a hug devoid of any emotion. Such is the unfortunate lot of those that are born with autism. For the uninformed, they are treated as less than normal and are subject to derision, misplaced anger, bullying, and misplaced sympathy. Their mistakes and efforts to live normally are often a laughing matter. They are often clumsy, shy, disruptive, loud, whiny, contrary, morose, disinterested, easily delighted, irritable, inattentive, manic, and every oxymoron word pair you can think of. They can either be bottomless pits of boundless energy, an annoying sight huddled in a corner, or a source of stress in every home. Yet, for those who love them and understand them, they will always be a part that, if missing, the family would not be considered whole.

Although studies have been conducted since the early 1900s, Autism, Autism Spectrum Disorder, and Pervasive Developmental Disorder are still big mysteries in the whole galaxy of medical disorders. Medical breakthroughs have been few and far in between but those successful few have shed a better light on the disorders and have made society respond in a far better manner towards persons afflicted with the disorders. Incidentally, technological advancement in terms of neurological research and studies, even those that are not specifically aimed at autism disorders, are beginning to untangle the mysteries surrounding the disorders, and some remedies have been discovered, many of which have improved the quality of life of those suffering from the disorders as well as their families. Still, many of the affected families are undoubtedly wishing for a complete recovery or phenomenal developmental cures. Although these wishes are still not yet within reach, living with autistic disorders is not as hard as it once was.

Along with the continuing efforts of the medical field to combat the disorders and mitigate their effects, the whole world is also making an effort to extend a helping hand and eradicate the apathy that was bordering on indifference that many people had taken in the past. The social landscape is changing and more doors are opening to these fellow members of our society that have fallen victims to the illness and some have even been given the opportunity to fully integrate into society and take part in community building.

This book covers topics that can help those who sincerely want to help their loved ones who are suffering from autistic disorders. Know that there is always hope and while this book is far from providing all the answers, it can serve as a guide to those who want to expand their knowledge on the subject matter. Sometimes a difficult situation can change for the better from just simply asking a question, looking in a new direction, stopping to carefully consider different options, or, in some cases, simply turning a new page.

AUTISM AT A GLANCE

Definition

In its classic definition, autism is described as a neural development disorder that is characterized by a difficulty in social interaction and communication. A person with autism may also display repetitive or restrictive behaviors. These days, however, the term autism is used side by side with autism spectrum disorder or (ASD). This text will use the term ASD to encompass autism as well as to encompass a group of complex brain developmental disorders that are characterized in varying degrees by both impairment of social interaction, social communication, restrictive behaviors, and repetitive behaviors.

ASD is a wide-spectrum disorder that includes:

1. Autistic Disorder
2. Rett Syndrome
3. Asperger's Syndrome
4. Childhood Disintegrative Disorder
5. Pervasive Developmental Disorder – Not Otherwise Specified (PPD-NOS)

Autistic Disorder

Recently described as "mindblindedness", autistic disorder is a neurological and developmental disorder which usually manifests itself during the first three years of life. It is linked to an abnormality in the biology and chemistry of the brain. A person with autism appears to live in his or her "own world" with little to no regard to others in the area. Often, there is a consistent routine usually comprised of repeating odd or peculiar behaviors, such as flapping of the arms or constantly rocking back and forth.

Symptoms

The following are symptoms typical of a child with an autistic disorder. However, it is important to note that some children may experience different symptoms than others. These symptoms may include:

- Impaired social interaction with others, even with their own parents.
- Dislike of physical contact. Autistic infants are often described as "unaffectionate" by their parents.
- Avoids making eye contact with anyone, even their own parents.
- Fails to make friends or interact with other children.
- Impaired communication with others.
- Late or no language development.
- Even if language is developed, he or she does not use it to communicate with others.
- Often repeats words or phrases repetitively like an echo (echolalia).
- Exhibits repetitive behavior.
- Has set rituals.
- Requires set routines.
- Is preoccupied with items such as lights and moving objects.
- Hates or is disturbed by loud noises.

Causes

The exact cause of autism is not known. In recent years, scientists have identified a number of rare gene mutations which may be linked to autism. A small number of these gene mutations have the sufficient ability to possibly cause autism on their own; however, in most cases, autism is likely caused by a combination of genes and environmental factors that affect the brain's development. Other possible factors suspected of possibly causing autism involve diet, digestive tract changes, mercury poisoning, or vaccine sensitivity. However, it is important to note that these suspected causes are still not proven, and the debate on whether they cause the disorder is very controversial.

Perhaps the most controversial claim is that vaccines can cause autism in children. One theory suggests that the MMR (Mumps-Measles-Rubella) vaccine may cause intestinal damage that can lead to developing autism. Another theory proposes that thimerosal, a mercury-based preservative used in most combination vaccines, is linked to autism. The medical community has disproved these theories; regardless, a group of parents and researchers still continue to disagree with them basing their beliefs on mostly anecdotal evidences.

Another recent report suggests the connection between the influenza virus and autism. A study in Denmark interviewed women while they were pregnant and then interviewed them again when their babies were six months old. They were asked specifically about what sickness they had (if any) during pregnancy and what drugs they took to treat them. Out of the 96,000 children born between 1997 and 2003, 960 (about 1%) were diagnosed with ASD. Mothers who said they had influenza while they were pregnant were more likely to have children who were later diagnosed with ASD, with the risk increasing about twofold. Mothers who reported to have had other infections such as colds, herpes, or urinary tract infections did not have an increased risk of having children with autism.

Essentially, this study showed that women who got sick with the flu were twice as likely to bear children later diagnosed with autism, while those who got sick for a long period of time (lasting a week or more) were three times more at risk. However, since this study was conducted, scientists have reassured pregnant women that not all women who get the flu while pregnant will bear a child who may be later diagnosed with ASD. For now, the link between influenza and autism is still unclear. In the meantime, scientists advise pregnant women to be on the safe side and get vaccinated against the flu prior to becoming pregnant.

Rett Syndrome

Rett syndrome is a neurological developmental disorder that involves the brain's grey matter. This disorder almost exclusively affects females (however, it can affect boys as well) and is characterized by a slowing of the rate of head growth as well as small hands and feet. Rett syndrome is usually discovered by the age of two, where in most cases the child will grow normally at first then begins to show signs of abnormal patterns in physical and mental development between 6 to 18 months of age. Rett syndrome was named after the Austrian pediatrician Andreas Rett who first described the disorder in 1966.

Symptoms

- Decelerated rate of head growth.
- Loss of muscle tone.
- Loss of purposeful use of hands; instead, habitual wringing or rubbing together of hands.
- Social and language skills deteriorate around 1 to 4 years old:
    - Stops talking.
    - Develops extreme social anxiety.
    - Withdrawal from or disinterest in people.
- Uncoordinated breathing or seizures.
- Stiff-legged gait.

Causes

In most cases, Rett syndrome is caused by a mutation of a specific gene ($MECP_2$) found in the X chromosome. It is believed that this gene may influence other genes that are involved in development, although what the gene does exactly and how its mutation can lead to Rett syndrome is still unclear. Although Rett syndrome is caused by genetics, in most cases the faulty gene is not inherited from either parent but, instead, is a chance mutation that happens in the girl's own DNA. There is no known risk factor for Rett syndrome other than being female. Rett syndrome is fatal in boys, mainly because they have only one X chromosome instead of the two that girls have. When boys develop the Rett syndrome mutation, they die shortly after birth.

Asperger's Syndrome

Asperger's syndrome (AS) or Asperger's disorder is similar

to autism in some ways but with an important difference: a child diagnosed with Asperger's syndrome has normal intelligence and language development. Also, unlike autism which can be detected by the first three years of life, AS is often diagnosed in children beyond the age of three, with most cases being diagnosed between the ages of 5 and 9.

Hans Asperger, an Austrian pediatrician, first described AS in 1944 when he noticed some behavioral patterns apparent in some of his patients, most of them male. Although these boys had normal intelligence and language skills, they manifested severely impaired social skills, poor coordination, and were unable to communicate effectively with others.

Symptoms

- Minimal or inappropriate social interactions
- Egotistical approach to conversations (talking only about himself)
- "Scripted", "robotic", or repetitive speech
- Lacking in common sense
- Awkward movements
- Odd behaviors and mannerisms
- Problems with writing, reading, or math
- Obsession on complex topics such as music or patterns

It is also notable that although a child with AS may exhibit good grammatical skills and an advanced vocabulary, typically they still manifest a language disorder in the form of difficulty in using language in a social context or having a tendency to being too literal.

Causes

There is evidence that points to AS having a genetic link such as the tendency for it to run in families. Researchers suggest that the genetic link with AS is much stronger than that of an autistic disorder inasmuch that it was observed that there is a higher incidence of family members to manifest AS-like symptoms or behaviors but in a much limited form such as slight difficulty in social interaction or in languages. However, scientists have yet to determine which gene or allele causes AS.

Another suspected cause AS is exposure to teratogens, which are agents that cause birth defects during the first eight weeks of conception. While this does not discount the theory that AS may be developed later on, it suggests that the disorder may arise very early in fetal development.

Childhood Disintegrative Disorder

Childhood disintegrative disorder (CDD) is also known as Heller's syndrome or disintegrative psychosis. It is a rare condition that is characterized by developmental delays in language, social function, and motor skills which manifest later in a child's life after a period of fairly normal development. The age at which this regression occurs can vary between the ages of 2 to 10. The regression can be so dramatic that the child may even be aware of it but does not understand what exactly is happening to him, only that it is apparent that his skills have suddenly become lost. CDD was first described in 1908 by an Austrian educator named Theodore Heller. He first called the syndrome *dementia infantilis*.

Symptoms

A child with CDD will show normal signs of development that is comparable with other children in the same age group. However, once the child reaches the ages between two to ten years, the skills he or she has developed will suddenly become almost completely lost in at least two of the six functional areas of development:

- Expressive language skills
- Receptive language skills
- Social and self-care skills
- Bowel movement and bladder control
- Motor skills
- Play skills

Impairment also occurs in at least two of the following areas: social interaction, communication, repetitive behaviors, and repetitive interest patterns.

Causes

There is still no known cause for CDD. Studies have shown a higher occurrence of epilepsy in children with CDD, but it is still not known whether the condition has anything to do with causing the disorder. CDD has also been associated with other conditions such as lipid storage diseases, subacute sclerosing panencephalitis (SSPE), and tuberous sclerosis complex (TSC).

Pervasive Developmental Disorder - Not Otherwise Specified (PDD-NOS)

While the list of conditions under ASD may seem to be clear cut, there are also children who manifest symptoms similar to the previous four disorders under the spectrum but do not meet all the criteria for a specific pervasive developmental disorder or for other disorders. This is where Pervasive Developmental Disorder – Not Otherwise Specified (PDD-NOS) comes in.

Often called Atypical Autism because the criteria for many of the autism spectrum disorders are not met (such as a late age of onset of the disorder or an atypical symptomatology), PDD-NOS is thought to be milder than the typical autistic spectrum disorders but such is not always the case. While some characteristics of the disorder may be milder, other characteristics can be more severe. It is also common for some children with PDD-NOS to have better social skills and lesser intellectual deficits when compared to other children with PDD-NOS.

Characteristics

No two children with PDD-NOS exhibit the exact same symptoms. Here are a few characteristics found in individuals who have PDD-NOS:

Social Difficulties

A child with PDD-NOS may want many friends but have trouble making friendships, especially if he or she also has language problems. Children with PDD-NOS may often have difficulty understanding body language, facial expressions, and/or tone of voice. Another common symptom of PDD-NOS is difficulty in understanding emotions (for example, being unable to distinguish whether a person is happy, sad, etc.)

Communication Difficulties

A baby with PDD-NOS may not babble. As a child, he or she can exhibit echolalia which is the act of repeating words or phrases over and over for no reason. Another common symptom of PDD-NOS is the inability to understand jokes or sarcasm. Children with PDD-NOS often take language too literally and have trouble "reading between the lines" (hearing sarcasm in someone's voice or rudeness, etc.).

Behavioral Patterns

Children with PDD-NOS may have emotional outbursts and tantrums often due to fear, anxiety, and/or the misunderstanding of a situation. They may also become dependent on routines and the need to have things to be performed in the exact same way each time. Children with PDD-NOS may also show a liking to dwelling on certain subjects, exhibiting an overwhelming obsession with talking about a subject they are interested in, and may only do activities that are associated with that topic.

Lastly, children with PDD-NOS may also manifest uneven skill development and have the tendency to have strengths in some areas while displaying delays in others.

Getting a Diagnosis

Problems in social skills, speech, and language, as well as restrictive activities and interests are signs that your child may have ASD. However, it is also important to keep in mind that although your child may have a few autism-like symptoms, it does not automatically mean that he or she has ASD. The diagnosis of ASD is based on the presence of multiple symptoms that disrupt your child's ability to communicate, form relationships, explore, play, and learn.

Here is a checklist that can help you determine if your child needs to be evaluated for ASD:

Social Skills

- Unusual or inappropriate body language, gestures, and/or facial expressions (avoiding eye contact, using facial expressions that don't match what he is saying, etc.).
- Lack of interest in other people or in sharing interests or achievements.
- Does not approach other people or pursue social interactions; tends to be aloof and likes to be left alone.
- Has difficulty in understanding other people's feelings, reactions, and/or nonverbal clues.
- Does not like being touched.
- Has difficulty in or fails to make friends with children of the same age group.

Speech and Language

- Delays in learning how to speak after the age of 2 or does not speak at all.
- Has an abnormal tone of voice and/or an odd rhythm or pitch when speaking.
- Repeats words or phrases over and over but does not show signs of intent to communicate with others.
- Has trouble starting or keeping a conversation.
- Has difficulty expressing needs and desires.
- Has difficulty understanding simple statements or questions.
- Takes what is said too literally; does not understand irony, humor, or sarcasm.

Restrictive Behavior and Play

- Repetitive hand movements such as flapping, rocking, etc.
- Obsessive attachment to objects such as keys and light switches.
- Has a tendency to be obsessed with a specific topic or interest, often involving numbers or patterns.
- Gets upset when there is a change in his routine or environment, has a strong tendency to put things in order such as lining up toys or following a rigid schedule.
- Often fascinated by spinning objects, moving pieces or parts of a toy; tends to be more interested in watching a moving part of a toy rather than playing with the whole toy.

If your child manifests a considerable number of the

above symptoms, than it is important to talk to your doctor about having him checked for ASD. You can also take online autism tests such as the M-CHAT (Modified Checklist for Autism in Toddlers) that asks questions about your child's behavior but keep in mind that the results should always be given to a doctor for a proper medical interpretation.

Getting a diagnosis for ASD may take a very long time. In fact, it can be after two to three years after the first symptoms were recognized that an official diagnosis is made. This is mostly due to concerns about incorrectly diagnosing a child; however, there are also instances where diagnosis is delayed because the doctor did not take the parent's concerns seriously or if the family was not referred to a proper health care professional who specializes in developmental disorders. If you feel that your doctor is not taking your concerns seriously do not be embarrassed by seeking out a second opinion from a doctor not affiliated with your current doctor's practice.

Some people with autism never get diagnosed but are able to live full and capable lives. For many, however, a proper diagnosis can give them many benefits. If you are wondering whether you should have your child checked for ASD, here are a few reasons why you should go to the doctor:

- It may provide a sense of relief for both the child and the family.
- If a diagnosis is positive, it can open up access to services that can help the child and the family that were previously unavailable to them.
- It can bring about a better understanding of how to deal with any problems that may arise.
- It may provide the family access to financial aid.

- It can get the family directed to a range of therapies and approaches that can help them cope with the condition.

If you are worried that your child has autism, it is highly important to get a medical diagnosis but don't wait for that diagnosis before you seek treatment. Remember that any early intervention during your child's preschool years will improve his chances for overcoming his developmental delays.

Diagnosing Autism Spectrum Disorder

Doctors need to look carefully at how your child socializes, communicates, and behaves in order to determine if he or she has ASD or another developmental disorder. The diagnosis will be based on the behavioral patterns that are revealed.

Diagnosis of ASD is complicated and will require a number of experts who specialize in this area, which is why you may need to ask your doctor or pediatrician for referrals. Specialists who may be involved in diagnosing your child may include:

- Child psychologists
- Child psychiatrists
- Developmental pediatricians
- Pediatric neurologists
- Speech pathologists
- Audiologists
- Physical therapists
- Special education teachers

The first phase of the evaluation is the parent interview wherein your doctor will ask for background on your child's medical, developmental, and behavioral history. You will also be asked about your family's medical and mental health history.

Next is a medical exam which includes a general physical exam, a neurological exam, lab tests, and genetic screenings. These exams are intended to determine the cause(s) for his or her condition and to determine if there are any other co-existing conditions. A hearing test is also conducted to eliminate possible hearing problems that may be the cause of social and language delays before ASD is diagnosed.

Your child will then be observed by specialists in various settings such as playing or interacting with people to see if there are any unusual behaviors that are associated with ASD. If behavioral patterns associated with ASD are observed, your child will then be screened for lead poisoning because lead poisoning can cause autism-like symptoms; therefore, it is highly recommended that children with developmental problems be screened for lead poisoning.

The following tests may also be included in the evaluation depending on your child's symptoms and their severity. These tests will also be helpful in determining what type of treatment your child might need.

Speech and language evaluation - a speech pathologist will evaluate your child's speech and communication abilities to check for signs of autism and look for any indicators for other specific language disorders.

Cognitive testing - a standardized intelligence test or an informal cognitive test may help differentiate ASD from other disabilities.

Adaptive functioning assessment - this includes social skills, verbal skills, and nonverbal skills as well as your child's ability to perform daily tasks such as eating or getting himself dressed.

Sensory motor evaluation - a physical therapist or an occupational therapist will assess your child's fine motor, gross motor, and sensory processing skills to check for sensory integration dysfunction.

Reacting to the Diagnosis

Getting an ASD diagnosis may be very emotional and upsetting for parents. A wave of emotions may wash over you: shock, denial, disbelief, helplessness, guilt, blame, and/or anger. For some people, these reactions may occur one after the other. For others, these emotions may occur all at once. One thing that is important to know is that you are not alone. There are many other parents who have walked in your shoes and have found a way to get through it.

While acceptance is the goal, the journey towards finding and achieving acceptance may differ for many parents. Some people may experience highly intense emotions over a long period of time, while others may experience less intense emotions but over a shorter period of time. Many parents often deny their own feelings and tend to focus on taking care of their children. However, that approach may result in exhaustion and feelings of being burnt out. It is important for you to recognize and identify your own feelings for the benefit of both you and your child. Take the time to grieve and recover in order to be able to achieve a greater acceptance of your situation.

The meaning of "Acceptance" is also different for many parents. It can mean believing that the diagnosis is correct or taking active steps in a positive direction to deal with the situation or both. Regardless, acceptance helps give you the motivation to move on and find the strength, energy, and courage to help your child.

GOING IN-DEPTH

Autism in Early Years

Toddlers with ASD manifest developmental delays, especially in their communication and social skills. While a normal child may start babbling by 16 months and can use meaningful two-word phrases by the age of 2, an autistic child does not. Nor does he/she make eye contact or respond to his/her name, which can make communicating with an autistic child very difficult. However, there are ways to effectively communicate with a child diagnosed with ASD, which will be discussed in detail in the next chapter. All you need is a lot of patience, understanding, and consistency. It is also important that you learn everything you need to know about ASD in order to properly care for your child.

If your child is diagnosed with ASD, the first thing you need to remember is to not expect your child to be like other children of his/her age; doing so will only give way to negative feelings of disappointment, guilt, and/or anger. Instead, accept your child wholly: quirks and all. To help you know what to expect, here is a list on how an autistic toddler behaves. A toddler with ASD usually:

- Does not use meaningful two-word phrases by 24 months, although he may repeat what he hears.
- Seems as if he is unaware of other people's feelings.
- Has difficulty engaging with others.
- Stiffens when someone touches, cuddles, and/or holds him.
- Has a robot-like or sing-song voice.
- Is often withdrawn.

- Does repetitive movements such as flapping hands, rocking, or spinning.
- Becomes extremely upset by the slightest change in routine.
- Spends hours lining up toys or other objects instead of playing with them.
- Can lose language or social skills he has previously mastered (especially for those diagnosed with CDD).
- Can show aggressive physical behavior.

It is a good thing to keep in mind that whenever your toddler shows physical aggressive behavior, it does not always mean he just wants to be disruptive and naughty. This aggressive behavior is usually brought about by the child's frustration of not being able to express what he needs and/or wants in other ways. When this happens, it is best to keep calm and try to calm him down while finding the cause for his tantrum; getting frustrated yourself will only make matters worse.

Another important thing you need to remember is that an autistic child is still a child nonetheless and what kids love most is playing and having fun. Both you and your child need to feel that there is something more to life than therapy. Find ways to have fun with your child by thinking of things that make him smile, laugh, and come out of his shell then schedule playtime when your child is most alert and awake. He is more likely to enjoy activities that do not seem therapeutic or educational. It should not feel like work but rather a break where he can enjoy time with you without feeling pressured to "do the right thing".

Having an autistic toddler also means devoting a lot of your time to your child as he will need special care. If you and your partner need to keep your jobs to support the family, then it is imperative to find someone who can provide care for your child either round-the-clock or just until at least one of you gets home. Some parents hire caregivers to take care of their child, while others ask relatives for help. Both can be good choices but also have disadvantages depending on the situation. Hiring licensed caregivers can be ideal as they are trained in taking care of the elderly and/or children with disabilities; however, they can be very expensive. Some parents may also be hesitant to hire people they don't know to take care of their children due to trust issues. On the other hand, while a relative such as a grandmother, an aunt, or a cousin may be a good choice, it is important to consider if they can handle different situations (e.g. if the grandmother is too old, she might not be able to handle your child when he becomes physically aggressive). You will also need to teach them everything they need to know about ASD, how to take care of your child, and what his quirks are. In addition, you might not be able to have anyone else attend regular checkups and evaluations for your child as some insurance policies require that both parents or one parent goes with the child to attend these regular visits to the specialists.

If for some reason the family cannot find someone to care for the child, then one parent must sacrifice his or her job in order to stay at home and take care of the autistic toddler, at least until the child is old enough to attend school. A parent needs to be physically, mentally, and emotionally prepared to accept this challenge as taking care of a toddler with ASD can be hard. On the other hand, being the one to take care of your own child has its own rewards such as being there whenever your child reaches a milestone such as learning a new word, eating by himself, or just being able to make sure that your child is cared for the way you prefer.

Because the job of taking care of an autistic toddler can be taxing, it is also important for the stay-at-home parent to take some time for himself or herself in order to avoid getting over worked or stressed. Resting your body and mind is important for the sake of you, your spouse, and your child. Getting stressed and/or exhausted must be avoided because you will not have enough patience and understanding if you are overly exhausted and/or stressed.

You must also remember to never give up. ASD may be an impossible condition to predict, but that doesn't mean that you can jump to conclusions about what life will be like for your child. People with autism, much like everyone else, have their entire lives to grow and develop their abilities. Being optimistic will also encourage your child to expand his/her limits.

Autism at School

Once your child reaches school-age, the dilemma of deciding what to do for your child's education emerges. At first, it may seem like a decision of whether your child should be home-schooled, attend a public school, or attend a private school. As you go along, you may find that the choices are not so simple, and you may feel confused with the choices. This section is intended to address this exact dilemma in order to help you make your choices.

To Home-School or Not

The first thing you need to think about is whether your child will be home-schooled. However, prior to that, you need to know that there is no single "right" choice for all children with ASD. It will still depend on how your child will react to the system. Some thrive in a more private setting at home while others do better when allowed to interact with other children of his age. Since you, the parent, are the one who knows your child better than anyone, it is best for you to look at each setting and decide which one is best for your child depending on his needs and quirks.

Here are the pros and cons of homeschooling:

PROS

- Homeschooling gives you the freedom to vary his program depending on his needs, moods, and interests. If something in your curriculum is not working, you can change it right away. Breaks can be given at any time that he needs it. He can also be indulged to his heart's content if he has a particular interest on a certain topic such as a color or an animal.
- A multi-sensory approach can be employed to its fullest in this setting as you and your child can act, sing, and dance out the lessons in whatever way you want to try.
- Homeschooling is a one-on-one (or one-on-two, if you have two children diagnosed with ASD) teaching approach. That means your child can learn his lessons at his own pace and have direct contact with his "teacher" if he needs anything.
- It gives you the opportunity to teach your child how you approach things in life. For example, not everyone tackles math problems the same way; some stick to the textbook approach while others find different ways to solve the problem. Homeschooling gives you a chance to share tips and tricks you have learned while you were at

school to make studying and learning easier.
- Homeschooling also gives you time to teach your child about your religion, whether you are Catholic, Christian, Buddhist, etc., without worrying about discrimination. It also allows you to teach your child the principles you adhere to when going through everyday life without worrying about outside influences.
- Homeschooling also shelters your child from discrimination and bullying which is often present at regular schools, resulting in less stress for your child.

CONS

- One of the most common arguments against homeschooling is the lack of interaction with other children of the same age. Homeschooling tends to isolate your child inside your home, so you'll need to schedule a separate time for socialization.
- Homeschooling is not always possible especially for families who have financial needs or have parents who are both working.
- Packaged homeschooling programs or curricula can be very expensive. While there are some that can cost little or are sometimes free, finding one can take a lot of time and research.
- It is also necessary to understand and comply with laws regarding homeschooling. While some places can be more lax towards regular reports, there are many places that require reports to be submitted more frequently. Although these reports may not be particularly difficult, it could require a considerable amount of time which many parents

may find hard to include in an already busy schedule.

If you are considering homeschooling your child, here are a few helpful hints and suggestions:

- Remember that homeschooling involves the whole family. Parents need to agree on the methods and strategies to be used. With enough worries and stress on parents because of having a child with ASD, it is not a good idea to add more stress by not being in agreement.
- If your child has siblings, then what are your plans to provide equal time for them? Some siblings may become jealous on the amount of time and attention you give on the home-schooled child, resulting in sibling rivalries. Make sure you have enough extra special alone-time for your other children.
- Join a homeschooling support group if possible. Joining one will provide you with help and advice from other parents. You can also get additional materials and ideas from there.
- Schedule alone-time with your spouse. It is important to have time alone with your spouse as a couple to maintain the structure of your marriage.
- Make plans to involve your child in social and community activities such as church activities, sports, etc. This allows your child the opportunity to interact with other children as well as adults.
- Trust yourself as a parent. Believe in what you do and that you know your child better than anyone else which entitles you to know what is best for him. Remember that homeschooling is not a lifetime decision. You can always change your mind

if this approach ends up not working for your child or your family.

Public Schools and Autism Education

In many countries, public schools are required to provide autism education, which can be a good setup for your child depending on his needs and abilities. Here is a list of settings you may find your child going into if you consider sending him off to school:

- Typical public school classroom with no special support (mainstreaming)
- Typical public school classroom with support (1:1 or adaptations)
- Part-time typical classroom, part-time special needs classroom setting
- General specific needs class
- Specialized public autism class with some mainstreaming
- Specialized public autism class without mainstreaming
- Charter school
- Cyber charter school

Here are the pros and cons for public schooling:

PROS

- Public school is free, which can be a big deal for families with financial problems. With regular checkups and treatments for your child, many families often cannot afford to pay for private schooling. Also, if both parents need to work to

- support the family, then public schooling is the best option for their child.
- Public schools can also provide your child with the opportunity to interact with other children in as typical a setting as possible. This can mean that as he grows up, he can learn to tolerate other people's quirks or at least get used to them.
- In some countries, public schools are required to provide autistic children with the proper support in as typical a setting as he can handle.
- Some countries, such as the United States, require each child in public schools to have an Individualized Educational Plan (IEP) wherein you and your child's team from the school's district will lay out plans that involve your child's goals, special needs, and benchmarks which will measure his progress. If your child is not moving forward, a meeting can be called to decide what to do next.
- There is no possibility for expulsion from a special needs program. This means that there is less pressure for your child to make huge progresses.

CONS

- Not all public schools provide the same exact support for children with disabilities. This means that your child is most likely to get adequate support depending on what your district defines as adequate support. Finding a good public school with the right support you want for your child might require a lot of time and research. There are also cases wherein you'll need to move to the particular district the school is in before your child can enroll which may cause problems for your

family.
- Letting your child enter public schools means opening them to the possibility of being bullied or discriminated. While bullying is discouraged in most schools, it is still yet to be completely eradicated in most systems.
- While there are schools that respond quickly to cases where a child with special needs is not showing progress, many schools take a lot of time before adjusting its settings to the needs of your child. Furthermore, because there are other students to consider, sometimes the school will wait for more children to show similar problems before they change their approach.
- Public schools can also have a higher teacher to student ratio, meaning there is less one-on-one time for your child as the teacher needs to accommodate all of his or her students.

Special Needs Private Schools

With the increased rate of children being diagnosed with ASD, special needs private schools are springing up in many countries. However, the majority of these schools only specialize in reading disorders like dyslexia, while a few accept children with ADHD. Although there has recently been an increase in acceptance by private schools of children with Asperger's syndrome, these special needs schools still tend to exclude children on the ASD spectrum.

Here are the pros and cons of letting your child enter a special needs private school:

PROS

- Special needs private schools have built into their curriculum full-day therapeutic interventions such as speech, occupational, and physical therapy on top of their academics. This means that not only is your child learning his or her academics, he or she is also receiving therapy at the same time.
- It allows your child to interact with children with the same condition, meaning more possibility for your child to find true friends who can understand what he is going through.
- Teachers in these schools are specially trained to handle children on the autistic spectrum. This means that you can have the peace of mind that your child is in the care of professionals who understands and supports him or her.
- Autism-only schools are often set up based on a specific therapeutic philosophy. These schools spend the majority of the day implementing philosophies such as behavioral interventions or relationship development interventions.

CONS

- Private schools can be very expensive, with tuition costs that can reach over $75,000 per year.
- Location can also be a problem. Because private schools for children in the spectrum are quite rare, it may be nearly impossible to find one in your local neighborhood. This means that there is a high possibility that your family might need to relocate in order to be near the school. Another option is to have him or her housed in a dormitory but that

means finding someone who can stay with him or her such as hiring a caregiver. This option also adds up to the expenses you'll need to cover in sending your child to private school.
- A school for children with ASD can also be a world unto itself, which means that your child will only have social experiences with people who understand and care for them. This can be a problem as it leaves your child unprepared to live in "the real world" where not everyone understands his or her condition.

Finding the Right School for Your Child

Now that you have an idea on the advantages and disadvantages of different educational options for your child, it is time to go school-hunting. The first thing you need to do is to research on possible school candidates. Joining a support group for parents of children with ASD can be a good idea as you can ask for advice and suggestions on which schools in your area or near your area have the best support for children with ASD. Once you have a list of possible schools, then it's time to go visit them.

Of course, it is very important for you to assess each and every school yourself as you are the one who knows best how your child behaves in different settings and what his needs are. However, like many things associated with ASD, this is easier said than done. Here are a few tips on choosing the best school for your child:

- Observe the school's atmosphere. Does it feel like your child will feel welcomed there? Do you feel like your child will be treated with kindness, care, and understanding there? How open is the school? Did you follow a strict schedule when touring the school or did the school administers allow you to roam freely and observe any classroom you chose?

- Observe the teachers. How are they interacting with the children? Having the right teacher can make a huge difference in your child's education. Even when the school does not have the right equipment necessary to help children with ASD, a good teacher should be able to improvise.
- Observe how the school interacts with the parents. Is there a limit on how often you can visit? Will you be allowed to drop by anytime to see how your child is doing in his or her class? How will the school communicate with you? Will they provide daily, weekly, or monthly notes regarding your child's progress?
- Ask about the school nurse. Is he or she trained to address the health and medical needs of children with ASD?
- Observe the school population. Does it have a small children-to-adult ratio? A smaller ratio means more one on one time with your child.
- Ask about the school's policy on bullying. What do they do when someone gets bullied? What happens to the bully? What do they do to make sure it does not happen again?

Finding the right school for your child can be a work in progress. Sometimes, the first school you choose may end up to be less ideal for your child than you first thought, which means going through the process of school hunting again or choosing a different educational approach for your child such as homeschooling. Remember to always take the time to make an informed decision. Of course, in the end, the best judge is your child and how he or she adapts and thrives in the school you chose.

Autism in Adolescents

If you have a child with ASD who has entered puberty, then you would probably have gone through the stresses of frequent checkups with the doctor or a specialist to ask if your teenager's ASD is becoming worse. In reality, these are often not cases of worsening disorders but the simple fact that they are becoming teenagers. Adolescence on its own can be very difficult on parents; mixing it with autism may turn it into a very volatile situation.

Normal teenagers, thanks to their hormones, are often more non-compliant, uncommunicative, moody, don't like to spend time with their parents, and never do things their parents want them to do. When children with ASD hit puberty, they experience the same hormonal activity as typical teens do, meaning they can become even more non-compliant, moody, and unpredictable. The only difference is that teens with ASD do not have the same outlet as normal teenagers do in which they can express themselves. As a parent, it is important to know how a teenager behaves, whether on or off the spectrum, so you'll know which of your teen's behavior is due to his or her condition and which is brought about by hormones.

Here are a few things every parent should know about teenagers in general:

- Teenage behavior cannot be blamed on chemicals, vaccinations, or genetics.
- While some teenagers become conscious of the way their body smells, others do not care either

way.
- Some teens like being orderly. Others claim to thrive in chaos.
- Teenagers do not learn good self-esteem by themselves. They often rely on acceptance from their peers for self-confidence.
- Teens like to make their own choices, which are often not the same as their parents'. They also tend to become aggressive if they are not allowed to make their own decisions or if they have their decisions vetoed by their parents.
- Being moody is normal for a teenager, as well as raging hormones and masturbation.
- They are often not hungry at the same time as the rest of the family.
- Self-regulation is a word that is often not found in a teen's dictionary.
- A teenager is often on the road to finding his or her own identity so don't be surprised to see your teen joining different peer circles every week. One week, your teen may decide that he or she wants to be one of the popular kids and then the following week he or she tells you that being non-conformist is his or her natural personality.

School can be a tough place for teens, especially those who are diagnosed with ASD. In junior and senior high school, conformity is the usual norm and is valued like gold. For teens with ASD, social conformity may be very difficult to achieve thanks to their condition. Often, bullying and discrimination intensifies as an autistic child turns into a teen. Most teens want to fit in but sometimes they simply don't which makes it a very difficult experience for them. Routine can also be hard to maintain as high schools often require flexibility since students will need to move from classroom to classroom, subject to subject, and teacher to teacher which can be stressful for teens with ASD who are used to structure and consistency.

Soul-searching is also an integral part of teenage life. Many teens begin to start looking for their path and purpose in life once they hit puberty. While parents cannot provide a specific path for their teens to follow, rest assured that they will find their own path eventually. While telling them that things will get better when they get older, it does not solve the immediate problem. The best thing a parent can do is to be there for their child every step of the way.

Some teens with ASD, especially those with Asperger's syndrome, attempt to be "normal" as a way to try to fit in. Conforming to the present norm dictated by most teens may look like the easiest way to becoming accepted in society. However, this can end up with your teen hating herself and feeling ashamed of who she really is. If your teen has things that she is interested in, don't undermine it by making your teen conform. Instead, teach her to use her talents and passions to find a niche in school where she can succeed, like a club or a group that is centered on specific interests such as the drama club where many quirky kids tend to find refuge. Sometimes the key to helping your autistic teen is to find people who can connect with your child. Helping your teen find a way to express her feelings is also a good idea as it can be the first step on relieving any stress your teen may experience during her years in high school. Once your teen finds a place in which she feels she belongs then she is on the way to finding self-acceptance and the path and purpose that will dictate the rest of her life.

Transitioning to Adulthood and Independence

Whether their teen is on or off the spectrum, most parents find it very hard to let go and give their teen more independence. This is even harder for parents with a teen diagnosed with ASD who have held their child's hand for a good part of his life; achieving the balance between holding on to your child and letting go can be one of the most difficult things a parent has to face.

Completely disconnecting yourself from your teen's life may be a bit harsh. Teenagers expect their parents to be in their lives and out of their faces at the same time. This means working on the sidelines or behind the scenes where your teen may feel you are still there when he needs you but at the same time far away enough away for him to be able to make decisions on his own. The best approach is to start by loosening your grip and watch how he will do. You may be surprised to find your teen to be able to meet the challenge of being independent. On the other hand, if he slips backward, you need to be ready to catch his fall while at the same time making sure it does not hurt your teen's ego.

Helping your teen transition into adulthood can be laborious and discouraging for any parent. Not only are you facing the reality of having to let your child, the one whose side you have always been on for most of her life, become independent, in some countries there are also laws and policies which you need to conform to as your child grows up.

Some countries require you to prepare a transition plan by the time your child reaches the age of 14 to 16. Transition planning allows you, your child with ASD, and her school system to begin preparations for the time when your child graduates and beyond. The process may include an introduction to your country's adult services and support that are designed to provide her with the skills necessary to succeed post-high school.

The first thing you need to do is to assess your child. What do you want her life to look like in the next 5 years, 10 years, and so on? What is it that you don't want your child's life to look like in the near future? What will she need in order to achieve goals and avoid failures? Know your child's strengths and weaknesses as well as what are her passions.

Next is writing short-term and long-term goals for your child. Think of it as a mission statement for your child's transition. These goals should be built from the information you have gathered on your child's assessment.

Lastly, you need to think of the possible obstacles your child may face in reaching these goals such as additional skills she may need in order to be successful or resources that may help her accomplish her goals.

A transition planning team includes:

- You, your child, and other interested family members
- Your child's transition coordinator
- Your child's special education teachers
- Administrators
- Psychologists
- Speech and language pathologists
- Other related service providers

You can also add other people whom you think would be

helpful in creating a transitional plan for your child. Finding a college course, a job, or a career for your autistic adult can be easy with the help of a good transition plan. Adults with autistic traits can also have an advantage when looking for careers. While a typical 9-to-5 work setting may not work for most adults with ASD, there are many other careers where they can be perfect candidates.

One common trait for those with ASD is their failure to see the picture as a whole and instead tend to focus on specific parts of the picture. While this can be a problem in most settings, it can be a valuable trait in careers such as an astronomer where you need to look for deep space anomalies or as a lab technician where you need to look for unique cells. Other careers perfect for this attribute include biological researchers, antiques appraisers, and art historians.

For adults on the spectrum who have an obsessive need to follow rules, perfect careers include ones in the military, in hospitals, or in laboratories wherein following the rules is crucial. If your autistic adult likes animals but not people, then he should find a career that is animal-oriented such as working on a farm, in a zoo, or in a veterinary clinic. Those who think better in pictures but have a hard time understanding conversations can find a career in areas like CAD (computer aided design), architectural model construction, etc.

The key to a successful adult life and career for your child, whether on or off the spectrum, is to find and support his passions and encouraging him to get the appropriate training to enhance his abilities. Keeping an open mind is also important in order to be able to find possible careers for your child.

LIVING WITH AUTISM

People get sick all of the time; that's a fact of life that, although we would have liked it to be untrue, is nonetheless as inescapable and as certain as death and taxes. Unfortunately, parents of children with ASD get to suffer the anxiety, apprehension, stress, and other similar predicaments of other parents at almost twice the level of difficulty. There is not that wide a difference to the common ailments that children, regardless of other underlying condition, suffer. However, those with ASD have exacerbating factors associated with communication and social skills; thereby, making even their simple conditions worse than they should be.

Other children under normal conditions can generally explain what ails them, although at varying degrees of clarity or certainty. They can communicate any discomfort that could lead parents to discover if other more serious conditions are present. The only course of action for parents of children with autism is to hover over them constantly and be observant of even the smallest of details. Parents have surprisingly enormous patience when it comes to their child but if they do not know what to look for and what to expect, no amount of diligence and attentiveness can save them from grief later on. This chapter presents situations that should be mentally marked so in the event they come, you will be ready to handle them or at least be a little less panicked and disorganized.

Before an in-depth look at these potential health problems, we should identify those behaviors that commonly occur in persons with ASD so that we can isolate those that could mean serious illnesses from those that arise from simple idiosyncratic manifestations. Remember that persons with autism lack normal communication skills, and they are generally loners. Therefore, it goes without saying that their attempt at reaching out and conveying their emotions could be limited to grunts, moans, crying, whimpering, or just staying unusually quiet. This could pose a problem if we are not equipped and ready to interpret what these actions mean. It might be cliché to say this but the only way to really tell if something is wrong is to keenly observe and to know your child's usual behaviors. Do not dismiss any change in behavior as a common result of his condition. Changes in behavior such as decreased appetite even with his favorite food, unusual irritability, acute weight loss, and/or self-injury means something could be seriously wrong.

The ironic thing is the same could be true if the child is doing unusually better. The key word here is 'unusual'. That is why it is important that you, the caregiver, or the doctor knows the child well so that these changes in him can be detected early and interpreted correctly. For the most part, there is no difference among children all over the world when it comes to healthcare. The things that we usually do for one child can be applied to another child such as making sure that she observes proper hygiene, does not ingest anything other than food, stays indoors during bad weather, stays dry, and sleeps well. Regular checking of temperature, ears, mouth, and limbs is also a must. These are ordinary things that should pose no problem except when dealing with a child with autism; these seemingly simple things can get from a little hard to awfully complex very fast if we do not know what to do. Take for example a routine check-up. It usually involves waiting at a clinic's lounge, reading some magazines, talking to the doctor, a little probing here and there, checking of temperature, enduring the cold touch of the stethoscope, some questions, and it's over. When your child has ASD or another pervasive developmental disorder, these actions can take hours and can prove to be stressful both for the parent and the child.

If the child's disorder is detected early in his life, it is important for parents to learn **preventive care** and to seek for a healthcare provider or caregiver that knows how this is done. This primarily prevents several complications to crop up later and gives the child and the physician or caregiver a better chance of getting closer to each other. In this day and age of specializations, it is hard to find a medical practitioner that can cover all the child's needs, so it is imperative that parents look for someone that truly understands their child's condition. It cannot be considered as a separate disorder and thus be treated by another doctor nor is it recommended that the child be brought to several other physicians for each type of sickness or medical condition. Parents should find someone that can be a dedicated, primary healthcare provider for the child: someone that knows and understands the child's difficulties. Bringing the kid to different clinics all the time is not the best way to go. There should be one place where the child can be comfortable and at ease. The key word here is familiarity. If it can be done, pictures of the clinic staff should be slowly introduced to the child so that the child can begin to understand that these are people who are there to help him. Within the child's daily routine, the activities and procedures such as the aforementioned checking of eyes, ears, mouth, and some other body parts should be introduced as some sort of a game. It might also be helpful to give the child toys that resemble those activities and instruments that can be seen in a clinic so that everything will seem familiar to him and, therefore, be less frightening.

For more able children (in terms of understanding and verbal communication), telling stories about the place and the procedures will also greatly lessen the negative emotions that could crop up. It is likewise good to let the child know that you will always be there throughout the entire process. Know the things that can calm or distract him. During all of these procedures, the parents and/or the primary caregiver should be informed of all of the procedures taking place. It is not acceptable to just let others take care of your child or believe that medical persons should know more about the medical conditions of your child than do you. As a parent, it is your responsibility to know and understand any and all procedures and medical conditions that involve your child so feel free to ask questions about the procedures and about the medications that are being performed or that are being recommended. Be aware of several options regarding these medications so have a talk with the pharmacist as well when you go to fill the prescription. If your child does not like a certain medicine's taste, most pharmacists can add special, non-toxic flavoring to make it better-tasting. In the case of a tight budget, maybe they can give you something that will not bust the bank. The main thing is that you should not hesitate to talk to anyone to know more about your options. If possible, talk to the doctor about his schedule. If an appointment can be arranged that can be done on less busy days, the better.

Chances are, even if you ensure to have only a few healthcare providers and medical practitioners around your child, there may be times that these people do not interact and communicate vital information with one another that should be shared. This is why you should always be informed as to the care, procedures, medications, and diagnosis of your child and verify that vital information about certain effects of treatment or medication has been relayed clearly to everyone involved in your child's care (i.e. school nurses, caregivers, doctors, nursing staff, pharmacists, therapists, etc.).

Emergency cases are another matter entirely as there may not be enough time for adjustments and 'acclimatization'. It is always best to scout out nearby health facilities and be aware of their locations, faster access routes, and certain emergency procedures. Again, it is pertinent that you talk to hospital staff (especially the ER staff) about their local system and learn more about how you can help, albeit unobtrusively, during any emergency situations involving your child. In some hospitals, it is their policy not to let outsiders in the emergency room or operating room; consequently, to avoid complications later on, inform them about your child's condition and ask them if they have anyone that can effectively deal with your child's situation especially the communication aspect. If they do not have personnel that can do that, request that they make an exception in your case. If that is not really possible, have a medical history summary that they can quickly refer to and be sure that it has all the important information about your child's case. Better yet, find a facility that can accommodate your child's special needs.

Dealing with Seizures, Regression, Sleep Problems, and Other Medical Conditions

Seizure (or Epilepsy) is one of the most common medical conditions related with autism and roughly 25 to 35 % of people with autism eventually develop seizures or seizure-like brain activity. Some of the medications that were reported to have better effects on seizures without affecting other symptoms are anti-epileptic drugs such as *Lamotrigine, Ethosuximide, Levetiracetam,* and *Valproic Acid.* There are also diets that seem to help (including the Atkins Diet, Ketogenic Diet, Gluten-free diets, and Casein-free diets) but are still under close study. It is also a good idea to outfit your child with a MedicAlert bracelet in cases when emergencies arise.

There is also another medical condition that relates to ASD that is called Regressive Autism or just simply called Regression. It is called such because the child appears to develop normally but then suddenly loses the previously acquired developmental skills such as speech, social skills, and/or social relatedness. This occurs commonly before the age of two just when the child is entering the most difficult stage of development. Some kids lose social development, language, or both. Studies involving this aspect of Autism are still not that conclusive; hence, some of the speculative linking of regression to vaccines that dates back to the early 1980s. There are no findings, however, establishing a causal relationship between regression and vaccinations. Experts even argue whether to consider this as a subset of the autism spectrum at all. What is certain, though, is that the condition exists and that we all should be aware of it. In cases where the symptoms manifest, call them to the attention of a specialist so that she may further evaluate the situation.

Getting children to fall sleep or making them stay asleep is a common problem of parents especially during the development stages. Luckily, infants do not normally fall under this category but when a child has ASD, the problem multiplies exponentially. The numbers are not consistent, and the situation varies from person to person, but typically sleep problems can occur more frequently in persons with autism (40 – 80%). Even with children without ASD, sleep is essential for their growth, mental development, and overall health. For children with ASD, a lack of an adequate amount of sleep can lead to irritability aside from its impact on the immune system and the child's overall development. It can also cause stress not only on the individual with the sleep problem but also on his caregivers and other family members. Needless to say, the overall mood of the entire house can be affected if everyone lacks ample shut-eye.

One of the most common reasons for sleep-related problems in persons with autism is environmental influences; another is accidental behavioral shaping. When trying to put a child to sleep, parents often have techniques like singing lullabies, rocking back and forth, and patting them on the back softly. After waking up, say in the middle of the night, these familiar patterns will most likely be absent so the child subsequently has trouble getting back to sleep. Children with ASD are also more sensitive to light, touch, and/or sound. There are some medications that can be taken such as melatonin, but the most effective way of dealing with this problem is observing the sleeping/waking patterns of the child so that you can adjust accordingly. It will probably involve a lot of trial and error at first but after discovering a routine that works, stick to it. Remove everything that can serve as distractions and never force a child to sleep. It is better to just let them discover their own circadian rhythm. Of course, working with experts in this field is a tremendous help so don't hesitate to consult one.

There are other medical conditions commonly associated with autism such as Fragile X Syndrome and Tuberous Complex Sclerosis simply because they both share symptoms with ASD and because some statistical data show a convergence at some point, but these are not direct effects of autism or the other way around. What is certain is that since it shows up, albeit in a small percentage among people with autism, there is a small possibility that your child might have these conditions as well, so it is not a bad idea to be prepared.

Dealing with Behavioral Problems

Children with ASD have trouble communicating although this is not necessarily a language problem. The main problem is getting the right message across. What we perceive as the associative meaning of words, gestures, and visual inputs might not always be what they see or understand so in their frustration to effectively connect to other individuals, they tend to isolate themselves. This same lack of connection to other people may lead to irritability, violence, and/or self-mutilation. This is not a hundred percent certainty, but it pays to know that it can sometimes lead to these situations if left unchecked. For the most part, they tend to just keep quiet. They do not respond to most stimuli like we do and will often appear nonchalant and unresponsive but that is not to say they have different needs and wants.

Chances are we just do not know how to ask them the right questions nor give them the answers they'd understand. What we interpret as reticence might just be a broken communication line between us so the best way to deal with it is to try to learn their language. Pay attention to details and see how they respond to certain situations, sounds, touch, gestures, and other stimuli. Remember their favorite games, toys, TV programs, foods, clothing, etc. Learn to distinguish their facial expressions, cries, moans, whimpers, shouts, and overall body language. Do not tolerate aggressive behavior; they might interpret it as "okay" if they are not taught differently. Most importantly, never show behaviors in front of them that you don't want them to emulate. As in any other situation, patience coupled with a little common sense, is imperative when dealing with behavioral problems in ANY child.

What You Need to Know About Medications

In dealing with disorders such as this, people have a tendency to opt for shortcuts or lean their hopes on non-proactive solutions like drugs/medication. Experts recommend these as a last resort because there are still a lot that can be done that pose no side effects and have more lasting effects but in severe cases where the limits of conventional care have been stretched, the medications listed here may be better options:

- **Naltrexone** – this medicine deals primarily with the effects/symptoms of the disorder but given the destructive nature of these symptoms, Naltrexone is almost invaluable. Clinical trials of this drug, at doses starting from .5 to 2mg/kg/day, showed reduction in self-injurious behavior, social withdrawal, stereotypy, hyperactivity, irritability, and agitation. However, it has a side effect called transient sedation.
- **Acetylcholinesterase Inhibitors** – due to the observed deficit in brain cholinergic function of autistic individuals, inhibitors were considered. Among these, the names Donepezil, Rivastigmine, and Galantamine rank high. Rivastigmine when taken twice daily at doses of .4 to .8mg led to significant improvements in speech and overall autistic behavior. Side effects are not few, however; they includes diarrhea, irritability, hyperactivity, and nausea. To counter these, one has to take Donepezil which in turn reduces irritability and hyperactivity at 50% effectiveness. Galantamine, on the other hand, enhances expressive language, as well as reduces irritability, social withdrawal, inattention, anger, and overall autistic behavior.
- **Alpha-2 Adrenergic Agonists** – these include

Guanfacine and Clonidine. Clonidine, when used transdermally, can reduce violent behavior, nighttime awakenings, hyperactivity aggression, as well as improves sleep, attentiveness, and overall mood. When used orally, it also improves problems with irritability, stereotypy, inappropriate speech, and oppositional behavior. Guanfacine, on the other hand, can improve attentiveness, hyperactivity, insomnia, and tics.

- **Oxytocin** – it has been found that certain polymorphism in the oxytocin receptor gene has something to do with autism so the use of a neurotransmitter can help improve repetitive behavior.
- **Cyproheptadine** – use of this drug can lead to a decrease in stereotypical behavior.
- **Famotidine** – this histamine-2 receptor blocker is said to improve certain symptoms in schizophrenia which shares similarities to some symptoms of ASD. Patients who took this drug in a study were reported to have improvements in communication, eye contact, social interaction, and a reduction in repetitive behavior.
- **Glutamate Antagonists** – it was observed that glutamatergic activity was excessive in some individuals with autism, so glutamate antagonists like memantine, amantadine, and lamotrigine were investigated. With amantadine, hyperactivity and inappropriate speech were reduced. Memantine is said to improve attention and social interaction while lamotrigine helped reduce seizures, stereotypy, and self-injurious behavior.
- **Cyproheptadine** – this drug is also said to help reduce stereotypical behavior as well as cause an improvement in expressive speech at a dose of

.2mg/kg/day in children.
- **Secretin** – administered intravenously, it seems to have no effect but when used transdermally, it helps to improve speech but only if not used in conjunction with other medication.
- **Antibiotics** – D-cycloserine is an antibiotic and a partial agonist at the glutamate receptor that seems to help lessen social withdrawal while another antibiotic, vancomycin, was thought to improve overall behavior.

Despite some improvements on test subjects, these drugs are not recommended by experts (at least not as a first option) as there are other choices out there that have longer-lasting effects and are not focused on the symptoms. However, there are cases where these medications help especially when used in conjunction with other healthcare remedies. Using these only as a last resort, parents should always consult extensively with experts in the field. Do not hesitate to speak with psychologists, psychiatrists, physicians, pediatricians, pharmacists, and nurses. Also, be reminded that when using drugs such as these, one should always weigh the benefits with the side effects and approach with caution.

Managing Sensory Issues

'Sensory' pertains to how we process information through our five main senses: sight, sound, smell, touch, and taste. It is through these senses that we accumulate knowledge about the world around us, interact with other people, and enjoy whatever experiences life offers us. In the absence of any of these senses, our ties with the world seem to come from a clogged information medium: hazy and incomplete. The newly-born, aside from forming her impression of the world around her from the stream of sensory inputs, learns of abstract ideas and emotions such as trust and caution. She becomes calm at a soothing voice, becomes agitated by loud noises, and is assured by a gentle touch. Sadly, people with autism do not get to experience these moments the way most of us do. They can either belong to one extreme end of the spectrum or to the other: meaning they filter sensory inputs differently by either being oversensitive or the other way around.

People with ASD not only react to the five sensory inputs separately, but they tend to interpret events differently as well. What others might find spectacular or amazing, people with ASD might find it bland or boring; conversely, they sometimes find ordinary occurrences rather overwhelming. This aspect of the disorder isn't just hard for the person with ASD but even more so for the parents in some instances. Imagine a child seemingly rejecting the touch of parents just because she finds it overwhelmingly painful. People with ASD sometimes look away just because they find looking at something disconcerting. As sad as this may be, some situations bear a closer look because they are potentially dangerous. Why? They tend to disregard warnings of caution just because they tend to ignore pain brought about by physical trauma, heat, or cold. That is also one of the reasons why some people with ASD seem not to care whether they hurt themselves; they do not feel the pain or if they do, they do not care.

There are some ordinary feelings that while others sometimes take for granted, seem so significant to persons with ASD. When autistic children suddenly cry for no apparent reason, they may just be uncomfortable with a certain fabric's feel on their skin or a certain pattern of colors on the wall or even just the rustling of leaves. The next time we interpret this as hardheadedness, contrariness, or willful behavior, we should examine it more closely. They might just be experiencing atavistic tendencies towards things that we find ordinary because their sensory filters have gone slightly awry. This is also the reason why they appear to be very wary when attempting even the most simple of activities. Their body's internal guidance system does not point where they want to go. Clumsiness and low dexterity can be a direct consequence of this, and shyness and intransigence can be additional side effects.

To know if your child has this problem, look for signs of:

- Repetitive behavior such as head banging, flapping of hands, and/or foot tapping.
- Poor eye contact.
- Short attention span.
- Poor coordination and handwriting.
- Avoidance or over reaction to touch.
- Trouble identifying objects by touch.
- Clumsiness.
- Lack of balance.
- Slow and repetitive speech.
- Lack of spatial awareness.
- Fear of movement.
- Fear of changing routines.

One of the earliest observable symptoms of ASD is a child's reaction to touch. If a baby tends to go stiff and cries when held or spoken to, she might have the disorder although this is not a guaranteed diagnostic tool. However, if this is the case, it will be very difficult for both the parents and the child. The first thing parents can do is accept the possibility of their child having ASD and avoid making the child feel unwanted or misunderstood.

Here are some tips from experts:

- Try to find a way to entice them to initiate the touch.
- Try to give them ample time to adjust to the possibility of a touch rather than surprising them with it.
- Start with a firm but unmoving touch instead of a tentative, light, and moving caress.
- After a firm touch, you can later move your hands after being certain that she is accustomed to it.

Parents can also minimize the unpleasant sensations by choosing fabrics that are softer than others. New clothes can have an unpleasant feel sometimes even to most people. You can lessen the effect of this by repeatedly washing new clothes first before letting your child wear them. Since they do not communicate well, parents should be patient in finding out their child's preferences. For those that are hypersensitive, there are techniques that work well like desensitization. If your child does not like crowds, try to patiently talk to her and say that you will just stand close to the crowd for a short period of time and then go away. After you see that she gets comfortable with just watching the crowd, try to bring her closer to the crowd the next time until you can have her mingling with the crowd more comfortably. It works the same way with rooms, sounds, or fabrics. Through all of these, explain to her what you are doing and assure her that you will always be there with her to allay her fears and lessen her discomfort. For those that belong to the other end of the spectrum (i.e. are less sensitive to touch, sound, etc.), understand that they sometimes tend to be less careless, like to engage in extreme sports or similar activities, and prefer activities that seem more dangerous to people without ASD.

Children with ASD may also play music loudly and shout more excessively compared to others. You may employ an occupational therapist that is very knowledgeable in these types of conditions to help, but nothing beats your constant guidance and understanding. Do not disagree with your child too much or prohibit him from doing what he likes. Instead, find a way for him to enjoy these activities without disturbing other people. If you can afford to, try to soundproof and/or child-proof the whole house. In addition, try to subtly encourage your child to try other less dangerous or noisy activities. It helps if your child sees you enjoying it, too.

Alternative Treatments

Previously in the book, the usual treatments of autism were discussed, but there are new and increasingly popular treatments emerging. They are not often mentioned because they either are not recognized by established medical communities as scientifically proven, they haven't gained universal recognition yet, or they are regarded as unconventional by medical practitioners. If you are concerned for your child, you will no doubt try to unearth every imaginable method known to man to help him, including those that are considered unorthodox. In this part of the book, some of the methods and medications listed and discussed are admittedly out of the mainstream list but if they can help lessen the burden, it doesn't matter if they are popular or not. As with the chapter on medications, it comes with a little warning: Proceed always with caution.

- *Chelation* – it involves removing heavy metals with medication. More specifically, this refers to the method of reducing blood lead concentration with the use of drugs such as calcium disodium edentate or oral meso-2-3-dimercaptosuccinic acid (DMSA). Believed to lead to better moods, behavior, and attention.

- *Immunomodulation/anti-inflammatory treatments* – sometimes the use of medicine like oral prednisone led to improvements in speech and developmental milestones.
- *Hyperbaric oxygen treatment* – HBOT may help persons with ASD because it is known to lower inflammation and improve hypoperfusion; both of these are reported to have been observed in persons with ASD.
- *Elimination Diet* – in the late 70s, it was proposed that casein and gluten malabsorption played a causal role in autism by altering neurotransmitter metabolism. Since then, various studies have been conducted observing casein and gluten-free diets. When removed from a person's typical diet, some foods like cow's milk, wheat, and corn were proven to have positive results. In other words, by removing some staple foods in a typical diet of a child with ASD may improve his condition. You should consult a nutritionist before attempting this to avoid complications.
- Taking *nutritional supplements* like:
    - Melatonin – for better sleep, communication, and play skills.
    - Carnitine – promotes better sleep, higher energy levels, and better expressive speech.
    - Tetrahydrobiopterin – better language and social interaction.
    - Vitamin C – lessening of stereotypical behavior like flapping of hands, pacing, rocking, and whirling.
    - Carnosine – improvements in overall autistic behavior and vocabulary.

- Multivitamin Mineral Complex – for overall health and circadian rhythms.
- Polyunsaturated Fatty Acids (PUFA) – it was learned in a study that persons with lower PUFA had more behavioral problems such as hyperactivity and temper tantrums.
- Piracetam – combined with risperidone, leads to better overall autistic behavior.
- Vitamin B6 and Magnesium – Vitamin B6 alone can improve speech and language in some children but has side effects like enuresis, irritability, and sensitivity to sounds. However, when Vitamin B6 is combined with magnesium, it has less of the aforementioned side-effects.
- Folic Acid and Vitamin B12 – some improvements in cognitive skills.
- Ginkgo Biloba – mild improvements in irritability, eye contact, and speech.
- Iron – better cognitive, motor, and social functioning.
- Probiotics and digestive enzymes – better autistic behavior but has side effects like hyperactivity and loose stools.
- Hypericum Perforatum – improvements in speech and less hyperactivity.
- Vitamins A, D, Zinc, and Calcium – children with ASD tend to stick to very few foods in the course of their lives and, as a result, have deficiencies in most vitamins and minerals. Giving them these will help lessen vitamin deficiencies and other physical defects later.

These dietary supplements and vitamins might not show

significant effects with regards to a child's autism but will greatly help in areas where the effect of these symptoms are significant like malnutrition, erratic circadian rhythms, and lower brain development.

- *Music Therapy* – constant music therapy of at least 1 hour a week is found to improve play skills and other autistic symptoms. By music, professionals mean anything that has something to do with organized sound and rhythm (singing, drumming, and piano playing). By bringing your child to music sessions, you may find him making longer eye contact and paying more attention to other activities. It proves how the universality of music can help even those that have difficulty processing the sensory inputs they encounter around them. Besides, it would probably be soothing to the parents as well so going to an occasional concert or two is not a bad idea.
- *Vision Therapy* – the use of ambient prism lenses may improve posture and hand-eye coordination. People who have ASD's difficulty in judging distances, being clumsy, and difficulty in learning could be sometimes due to their impaired vision.
- *Auditory Integration training (AIT)* – AIT involves listening to certain music filtered through a set of headphones to help reduce outside noise. It is said to improve irritability, stereotypy, and hyperactivity, and expressive speech.
- *Massage and Yoga* – aside from improved blood circulation and the relaxation of muscles, this can enhanced the emotional bond between parents and the child. Hence, it goes without saying that this should not be assigned to other people. The parents should at least learn the rudiments of proper massage for both the parent and the child

to enjoy the full benefits of touch therapy. This supposedly improves sleep and aside from the aforementioned emotional bond strengthening, the child's overall moods will improve along with lessening of stereotypy.

- ***Neurofeedback*** – this treatment leads to improvements in speech, better social interaction, and progress of cognitive skills.
- ***Vagus nerve stimulator (VNS)*** – treatment with the VNS can reduce intractable seizures which can be a great help if the child sometimes is in situations where he is left unattended.

Many of the remedies and treatments listed here, while considered generally safe, are not yet FDA approved. It is understandable that parents at the end of their rope may latch on to these as part of their last resort, but experts should always be consulted. One should always weigh the dangers against the potential benefits of any of these methods before proceeding. For those that are considered high-functioning autistics, it should be relatively safe to try any or a combination of these methods and it may even help but for those that are afflicted with a more severe case of ASD; however, some of these methods can be potentially harmful if not done correctly. As with anything else with regards to unproven methods, it is best to research thoroughly and choose something that is best for your child instead of just selecting one at random. It seems that a lot of these methods fall under the trial and error category, so it is best to tread carefully. After all, there are no shortcuts when it comes to your child's health and a couple of minutes more talking to healthcare practitioners can save you mountains of grief later on.

Managing Sibling Issues in the Family

If there are several children in the family and one of them has ASD, expect a lot of little *balancing acts* that would challenge even the greatest circus high-wire walker. If your family has several children of wide age gaps, this shouldn't pose much of a problem but if the age difference is not that great, then you should consider making a system or even just a simple scheme of dealing with the kids. There will always be the issue of immaturity even with the *non-afflicted* ones, and it is with **them** that a system should be built around not the one with the ASD disorder. This might sound a little off the mark and illogical but in the early stages of childhood, it is important that the non-afflicted child be treated with the understanding that his development will differ than that of the child with ASD.

This is more than matter-of-fact if you look at it this way: the ASD child's cognitive and mental development will be a little slower and trying to make him understand complex situations will almost seem like an exercise in futility. Needless to say, trying to make them understand complex situations will have to be undertaken really slowly to match with their concept of reality. On the other hand, the other child or children will have thousands of questions begging for answers, and it would be wise to deal with them immediately.

At the very start of learning that one of your children has autism, prepare the other children at once and if it is within their level of understanding, explain to them how their sibling and their sibling's behavior, thought process, level of maturity, and needs are different from theirs. Include them in a system in which they play active roles in caring for their sibling so that they understand that they are not just mere observers who are governed by a different set of rules. They may have to learn to adjust early on to their sibling's mood swings, lack of communication skills, apathy (in some cases), obsessive behavior, and unconventional thought processes. In turn, reinforce how proud you are of your non-ASD children on how well they are helping both you and their sibling and explain to them that by doing this, it is developing their own sense of empathy and understanding of other people, which are values that people respect and look for in others. There is almost always jealousy issues amongst siblings. Try to avoid favoritism in fanning the flames so to speak. It will appear (especially if you are really dedicated in caring for your special child) that you prefer one child over the other since you pay more attention to him, you spend longer time trying to teach him, and may appear more patient with him. Make sure you offset these actions and help prevent sibling jealousy and rivalry by doing special things with your other children as well.

Help your other children understand why it is so important that they try and embrace their sibling and minimize jealousy and rivalry. Perhaps explain how they are luckier in not having to undergo the hardships that will surely weigh their sibling throughout their sibling's life and that by developing these coping strategies now, they will be able to help their sibling in the future as well. While it is normal to provide special attention to the child with a disorder, try to do so in a way that doesn't alienate the children and create resentment. Don't expect the non-afflicted children to understand right away their roles and responsibilities in caring for their sibling; remember that they, too, have their own needs. Perhaps find out which roles and responsibilities they **enjoy** doing with their sibling and concentrate on those. Do not expect them to sacrifice their own childhood just to maintain their sibling's needs even if it is for their less fortunate sibling. By letting them choose which roles and responsibilities they enjoy helping with, they will feel as if they are an active participant in their sibling's care rather than a forced servant. In the meantime, make time to allow them the freedom and carefree way of life that only a child can truly experience.

Once that task has been organized and agreed upon, it is time to plan for specific activities that focus on bonding, interaction, and communication amongst the siblings. There are several games that can foster closeness and understanding, and those are the ones that you should introduce to your children. Even simple games that allow them to touch, see, and hear each other is a great way to strengthen their bond through sensory reinforcement. Focus more on the overall experience rather than on the goal or mechanics of the game (i.e. winning or taking sides). Instead, reinforce the ideas that the goals of spending time together or to have fun and become better friends. Make sure you limit the time of these activities to just short ones per day so as to not overwhelm your child with ASD; however, if your child with ASD is still enjoying and interacting with his sibling by all means let them continue to play. You should also allow each child to do activities separately with you as well in order to create the feeling of specialness and closeness they feel when getting to spend individual time doing activities with you as well.

Don't ever force your children to be together if they do not want to at a particular time. Rather, subtly involve them in situations that don't seem contrived or forced. You should also closely monitor and research the limitations and inclinations of your children so that you can more effectively plan activities that they enjoy doing together. Do not assume, like you would assume the other child to understand, that the ASD child does not comprehend what you want him to do. It just takes the right combination of signals to get the message across so try to explore the limits of their understanding, too. This way, you can tailor your family activities in such a way that everyone feels they are on common ground. As children grow, however, expect that the non-ASD children might want to spend more time on their own or with their own peers. This may be true for the child with ASD as well. Accept this as a possible eventuality but be assured that because you have guided, nurtured, and taught them when they were children, the bond they have as siblings will always be there.

BEING PROACTIVE

Standing up for your child who has ASD may not be easy. Most of the time, you may be faced with discrimination, bullying, and systems that need to be restructured in order to better accommodate children with ASD. Becoming an advocate for your child may mean more additional tasks on your to-do list but for most parents, the effort is worth it to ensure that your child is getting the treatment and support she deserves.

While on the journey to fighting for your child's rights, you are likely to find other advocates. Parents are the natural advocates for their children as they are the ones who have their child's best interest at heart. However, there are also others who join in the fight for the rights of children with disabilities even if they have no children of their own.

Here are a few children advocate groups:

- **Lay advocates.** They use their specialized knowledge and expertise to help parents resolve problems within the school systems. They often act on the child's behalf and are knowledgeable about legal rights and responsibilities.
- **Educational advocates.** They evaluate children with disabilities and make recommendations about services, supports, and special education programs. Often, they negotiate for services on the child's behalf.
- **Teachers and special education providers** are advocates as they provide support to children and their families. However, because they are employed by the schools, they may have limited ability to

advocate for children as it may put their jobs at risk.

You might be asking exactly what is it that advocates do? First of all, advocates gather facts and information that helps them learn about the child's disability and educational history which will then be used to resolve disagreements and disputes within the school. They also orient themselves about the school district's system so that they know how decisions are made and who makes them. Advocates are also well-versed in the legal rights and what procedures parents can follow to protect their rights and their child's rights. They are not afraid to ask questions and can define and describe problems in all angles, using their knowledge to develop strategies. Lastly, advocates are negotiators who are always seeking a "win-win" solution that will satisfy the interests of the parents, the child, and the school.

Being an advocate requires a lot of time, patience, research, and sometimes a sharp learning curve. However, with enough motivation, you can find your way in making a difference in the fight for your child's rights.

Here are a few tips to becoming an advocate for your child with ASD:

1. Be an expert on your child's condition. Read everything you can find about ASD. In order to be taken seriously as an advocate for your child, you have to know the facts about everything from the initial diagnosis of ASD, the various treatment options for ASD, the different educational choices, and your country's laws for protecting individuals with disabilities. You will also need to familiarize yourself with the medical and legal jargon and abbreviations associated with ASD.

2. Take the front seat. Being an advocate means you have to take the lead and become responsible in fighting for your child's rights. Becoming a leader will bolster your position in encounters with doctors, teachers, therapists, and other people whose services you may enlist in order to assist you and your child. Speaking with authority will also encourage service providers to take you more seriously.
3. Always consider the pros and cons of every option before making your choice. Weighing the advantages and disadvantages of each option will help reduce poorly made choices, especially in times such as choosing the educational approach you want for your child.
4. Keep your documents organized, from your child's initial diagnosis, doctor's appointments, medical bills, as well as paperwork and regular reports from your child's teachers, therapists, advocates, and doctors. This gives you the ability to produce necessary documents when the opportunity requires it such as a billing disagreement, a discrepancy between doctors' treatments, or if you need to switch to or enroll a new person in your child's care.
5. Find opportunities to educate others about ASD. This will not only help those around you and your child to understand her condition better but may lead you to meeting others that can provide invaluable information to you. Most importantly, it not only will make you feel good to help others, but it will show your children the importance of not only advocating for those you love but the importance of loving and advocating complete strangers as well.

Becoming an advocate can be hard work. However, you must remember that you are not alone and that there are many other parents out there who are either going through or have already gone through the same issues you are experiencing. Support groups and organizations for ASD are available all over the world. Joining one provides you with more resources you will need for your advocacy. Other parents of children with ASD can also provide good advice as well as tips and tricks that can make your job easier.

Organizations include:

- Autism Speaks and The Autism Society of America for those living in the United States
- National Autistic Society and Parents for Early Intervention of Autism in Children (PEACH) for those living in the United Kingdom
- The World Autism Organization which is an international organization.

Most of these organizations can be found via the Internet and provide many great resources that help parents better understand ASD.

FAMOUS PEOPLE WITH AUTISM

Human history is rich in stories of duality. It is a common theme of the continuing saga of man. For every epic war story, there are novels on peace and the struggles to attain it. These records of the world's spinning and turning are full of cycles running through joy and sadness, fear and valor, adversity and triumph but none is more inspiring than man's battle with himself and the very obstacles that are strewn in his path. While there is more to life than the implications of a Greek tragedy, imagine these individuals tackling herculean tasks everyday of their lives or imagine them in the backdrop of Sisyphus (minus the inappropriate back story, of course) and managing to push that proverbial giant rock of their disorder over the top of the mountain. Here are some who drew the hypothetical short stick but ended up with stories far larger and inspiring than all of us "non-ASD" people could hope for.

Satoshi Tajiri

There are very thin lines that separate the levels of normalcy amongst individuals and between those levels are realms that separate mediocrity from greatness; it just takes a little bit of luck and a little dose of genius sometimes to cross over from one plane to the next. Such is the case of Satoshi Tajiri, one of the legendary video game creators of all time. He has been diagnosed with Asperger's Syndrome – one of his symptoms manifested as an intense fascination with bugs and insects. He often neglected schoolwork as a child in favor of his bug collecting hobby much to the consternation of his parents. Indeed, while he wanted to become an entomologist, he didn't get to go to a four-year college or university. Instead, he attended a technical college and studied electronics for two years before eventually starting a game fanzine called Game Freak.

This fascination with games might have also been due to his neurological condition (one that led him to keenly focus on only one activity at a time). He became so engrossed with playing arcade games that he very nearly failed to graduate from high school. There is one story that tells of how he dismantled his Famicom (a Japanese computer) to learn how it worked. These three factors in Tajiri's life combined to make him into one of the saviors of the video game industry. His extreme fixation with bugs, video games, and electronics led to the creation of one of the most successful franchises in the video game industry: Pokemon. It was said that while watching two linked Gameboys one time, he imagined bugs crawling across the linked cables... and the rest is history. While the niche in which he found himself in the industry is just a tiny part, the revolution it created went on to revitalize a declining business and spawned a multi-billion dollar resurgence of one of the most influential social and entertainment force around the world. Who says a bug can't leave a giant footprint? Not Satoshi Tajiri, apparently.

Jason McElwain

Jason McElwain was a high-functioning autistic. Throughout his childhood, it was a struggle to maintain a normal social life and only in his teens did he begin to mingle and try to connect with other people. He was in a special education class and only his obsession with basketball kept him in contact with other people other than his immediate family and tutors. He would always shoot hoops for countless hours and practice some moves until he got too tired to continue. This is a sport that was introduced to him by his brother Josh, and it appeared as though his simple routine of going to the basketball court to play would be an endless and monotonous cycle until he found some other activity to fixate upon; that is until Coach Jim Johnson of the Athena Greece High School basketball team decided to give him an opening to be more than others could only hope him to be: he allowed him to function beyond his single-minded preoccupation and be part of a team as a manager. His role in the sport that he loves grew to encompass taking care of equipment, gear, and oversee the team's needs. Little did everyone expect that this autistic child's existence, whose presence on the court was as commonplace as the staccato sound of balls hitting the parquet floor, would expand to touch an entire nation as well. The window of opportunity for Jason McElwain occurred in a mere four minutes of his seemingly mediocre life.

It was the last game of the season, and Coach Johnson promised to let McElwain play if they were in a comfortable enough lead going into the end of the game. The Athena Greece High School basketball team was up by a double digit lead with four minutes remaining in the game, so Jason got his chance. Missing his first two attempts, he unleashed a salvo of deadly shots from beyond the arc and scored a blistering 20 points in that little time given to him. This elevated him to instant celebrity status and from there he went on to meet then US President George W. Bush, got interviewed on national TV, got to write his life story, was offered by major movie outfits for the rights to immortalize him on film, edged out Kobe Bryant's 81 point game for the Best Moment in Sports in 2006, be a commercial model, have a song written about him, and be a spokesperson and fund raiser for ASD persons all over the world. Those four minutes didn't just transform him but eventually changed all the lives that he was able to touch. Not bad for someone who only wanted to just play the game he loves.

Daniel Tammet

Some might call it an oxymoron to call an ASD person a genius, but Daniel Tammet's life is so full of these little contradictions that it might be possible that he is on an altogether different plane than the rest of us. Imagine someone some people would consider as having a neurological disorder eventually making a study on how the mind works. That can truly be mind-boggling if you care to think about it. However, Daniel Tammet did just that with his book Embracing the Wide Sky: A tour Across the Horizons of the Mind. Those who have observed him closely say that he has an uncanny ability to dissect the mind's functions and describe the processes with regards to sensory processing, social interactions, and language. Some might consider being called a person with ASD derogatory but if it meant being grouped with Tammet, it would be an honor. He is considered by many to be one of a handful of living geniuses on the planet today. He rose to worldwide acclaim after writing the New York Time's bestseller Born on a Blue Day; his autobiographical book. In 2004, he further astonished the world by reciting the popular mathematical constant (of which most people can only identify up to less than ten decimal places) Pi up to 22,514 decimal places from memory. He did this in 5 hours and 9 minutes and set a new European record. He is considered a "Brainman" (as his friends and close acquaintances call him) indeed in more ways than one and on several language games.

A FEW WORDS IN CLOSING

Sometimes for the "non-ASD" person, a headache is an incapacitating condition. Even a simple bruise is sometimes devastating. For persons with ASD, especially those afflicted with severe case of the disorder, their whole lives are one big headache and one eternal bruise...and yet, they continue to fight and struggle to survive and march to a rhythm nearly unfathomable to others. It may be extremely difficult getting hurt just by a simple ray of light, be discomforted by the rustling of leaves, or sit through a joyous occasion unmoved and unconcerned but they somehow manage. It might just be that the ones who should be taking lessons on how to overcome obstacles are those of us not afflicted by ASD. In our own limited understanding, we see a person struggling to read the alphabet, grappling with simple math, awkwardly buttoning a shirt, or coloring a drawing of an apple blue. We see a person less than what we think they should be. Sadly, what we are forgetting is to infer from these images we see is someone who is fighting a difficult battle...and winning.

The medical field is slowly but surely expanding to make this group of disorders seem less baffling. The whole scientific community is still tirelessly joining hands with parents everywhere to try and make an impact and/or find a cure. With all of these developments, one should always look at the horizon with hope that someday all families will be rid of the terrible weight that these disorders put on them. Sure it has taken slow steps to get to where we are now in understanding these disorders, but the constant struggle against it is still going strong.

Thanks to the efforts of caring parents, scientists, doctors, and activists, ASD is not as debilitating as it was before. The patience and diligence of everyone in trying to fully understand ASD is the reason why we see now see so many successful, high-functioning persons with ASD. The presence of these notable personages in the field advocating for wider understanding and raising awareness has made an exponential impact. While the medical world is still learning about and trying to treat and/or cure the illness, the rest of the world is learning to cope with it and help lessen its symptoms. This societal growth has eventually brought about the view that the disorder is not a permanent chain dragging the person down but a minor weight that, while it manages to slow one down, cannot keep him rooted in place for long. The fight against autism is far from won, but we are winning enough battles to say that we can overcome its more damaging effects.

For those who think that struggling against it is hard, many would surely agree. Yet with those many hands everywhere that are willing to extend help, it shouldn't be as hard as it sometimes feels. People with Autism Spectrum Disorder or its offshoots (whichever level of the disorder they might have) are members of our community that need more of our tolerance, patience, advocacy, and understanding rather than just our sympathy, empathy, or commiseration. People afflicted with ASD are fighters who deserve our respect and salutations. After all, we should not be defined by our medical infirmities but by our ability to overcome them.

Printed in Great Britain
by Amazon